LIVERPOOL
ROMA
CAMPIONE D'EUROPA
LIVERPOOL F.C.
SUPPORTERS ALL OVER THE WORLD
LIVERPOOL
THE PRIDE OF MERSEYSIDE
LIVERPOOL
adidas
Carlsberg

£5.25

Jamie Redknapp, former Young England captain and Liverpool International Supporters Club first-ever Player of the Year.

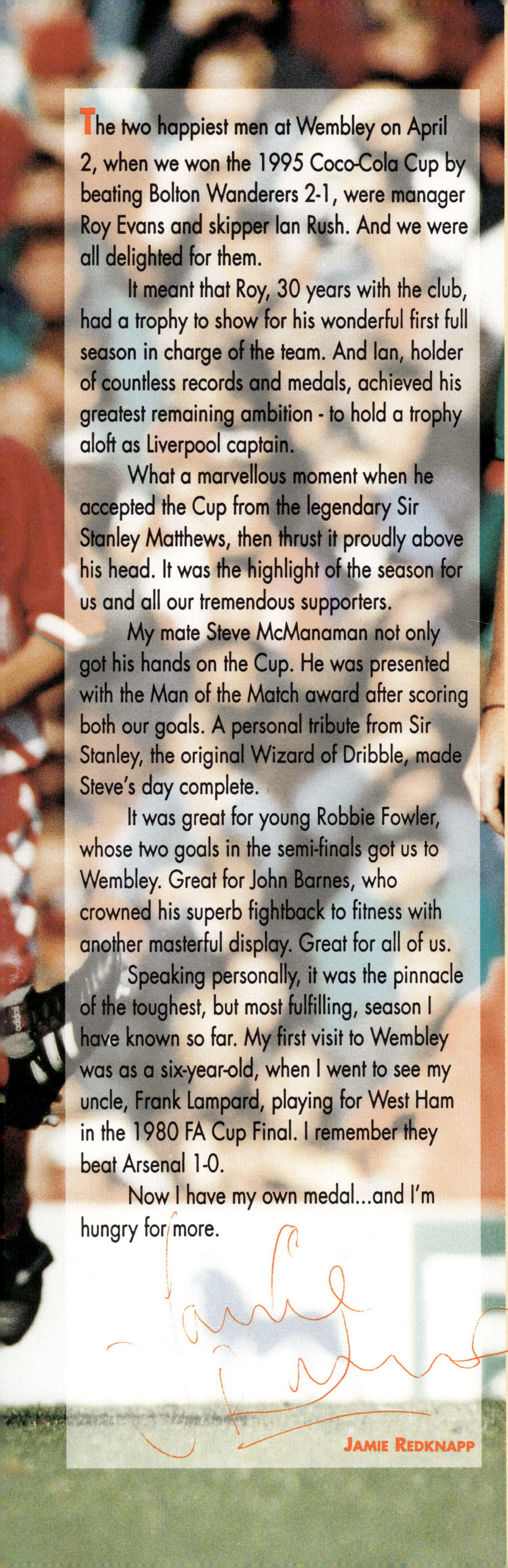

The two happiest men at Wembley on April 2, when we won the 1995 Coco-Cola Cup by beating Bolton Wanderers 2-1, were manager Roy Evans and skipper Ian Rush. And we were all delighted for them.

It meant that Roy, 30 years with the club, had a trophy to show for his wonderful first full season in charge of the team. And Ian, holder of countless records and medals, achieved his greatest remaining ambition - to hold a trophy aloft as Liverpool captain.

What a marvellous moment when he accepted the Cup from the legendary Sir Stanley Matthews, then thrust it proudly above his head. It was the highlight of the season for us and all our tremendous supporters.

My mate Steve McManaman not only got his hands on the Cup. He was presented with the Man of the Match award after scoring both our goals. A personal tribute from Sir Stanley, the original Wizard of Dribble, made Steve's day complete.

It was great for young Robbie Fowler, whose two goals in the semi-finals got us to Wembley. Great for John Barnes, who crowned his superb fightback to fitness with another masterful display. Great for all of us.

Speaking personally, it was the pinnacle of the toughest, but most fulfilling, season I have known so far. My first visit to Wembley was as a six-year-old, when I went to see my uncle, Frank Lampard, playing for West Ham in the 1980 FA Cup Final. I remember they beat Arsenal 1-0.

Now I have my own medal...and I'm hungry for more.

JAMIE REDKNAPP

# CONTENTS






*Written by* Bryan Webster.

*Photography by* John Cocks.

*Designed by* S. Bartram.

All facts believed correct at the time of going to press.

Published by
**Grandreams Limited**
Jadwin House,
205/211 Kentish Town Road, London,
NW5 2JU.

Printed in Italy.

There was no hint of the excitement to come as Liverpool's faithful supporters waited for the start of last season. Great changes were taking place and they were uncertain what to expect.

The Kop - the most famous crowd section in the world and the heart of Anfield - had gone, pulled down after an enormous send-off party at the last home game of the season.

Since the 1960s the Kopites had sung and danced as Bill Shankly's mighty Reds, and teams under the managers who followed him, piled up a record-breaking haul of trophies.

They sang and danced again at the Kop's farewell, turning it into a carnival with amazing costumes, dyed hair and a forest of flags and banners. But after a disappointing campaign, some couldn't help wondering whether things would ever be the same again.

They need not have worried. The job of reviving the Reds had been glven to Roy Evans, who had stood on the Kop as a youngster, signed for Bill Shankly as a teenager, then settled in his 20s for a future wlth the backroom staff.

For years he had shared in the tradition of sitting in the Boot Room, where the team and tactics were discussed endlessly by the managers and their staff. Now he was ready to launch the team into a new season for the first time.

They got off to an explosive start, famous new players were bought and, above all, the team played with their legendary passing game. This book tells the story of the season in whlch the Reds were reborn.

CПAPTAK
LIVERPOOL

adidas

LIVERPOOL
FOOTBALL CLUB

LFC

# The YOUNG GUNS

## -STEVE McMANAMAN

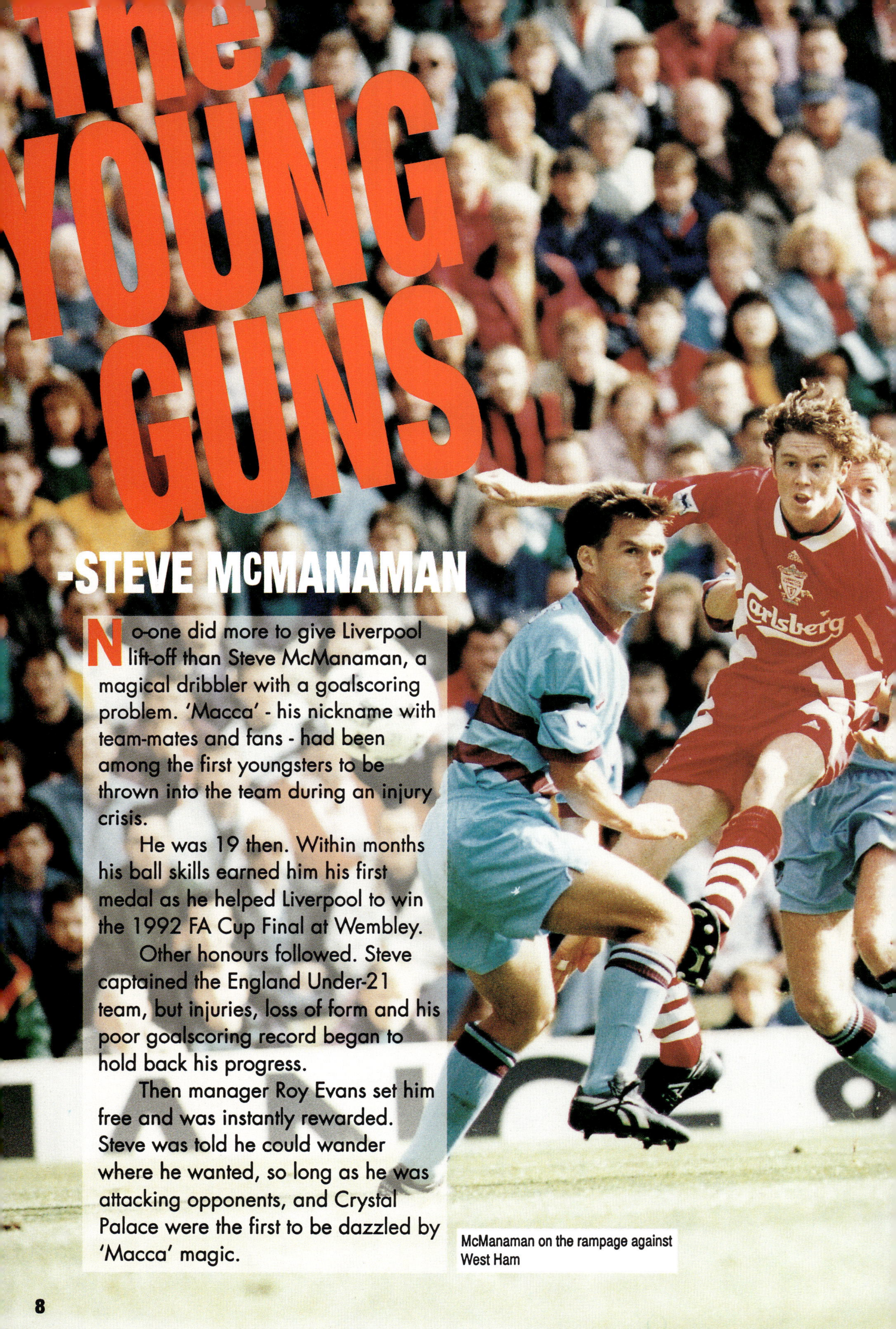

No-one did more to give Liverpool lift-off than Steve McManaman, a magical dribbler with a goalscoring problem. 'Macca' - his nickname with team-mates and fans - had been among the first youngsters to be thrown into the team during an injury crisis.

He was 19 then. Within months his ball skills earned him his first medal as he helped Liverpool to win the 1992 FA Cup Final at Wembley.

Other honours followed. Steve captained the England Under-21 team, but injuries, loss of form and his poor goalscoring record began to hold back his progress.

Then manager Roy Evans set him free and was instantly rewarded. Steve was told he could wander where he wanted, so long as he was attacking opponents, and Crystal Palace were the first to be dazzled by 'Macca' magic.

McManaman on the rampage against West Ham

On the opening day of the season, the tall, slim winger who hadn't scored for nearly a year got two of Liverpool's six goals and went on to prove himself one of football's outstanding entertainers.

Left-backs had always found him a bit of a handful, but now defenders on the right and in the middle also had cause to fear this speedy attacker who ran straight at them with the ball, then slipped away like a ghost.

"I used my own judgement and liked the variation of the new role," says Liverpool-born Steve. "I went wherever I thought that danger could be caused."

England manager Terry Venables made a point of watching him and liked what he saw. 'Macca' was called into an England squad in October, but did not play against opponents Romania.

A few weeks later, however, he was called on as substitute for most of the game against Nigeria and performed well. "I didn't feel strange at all," Steve recalls. "After all, there were three of my mates out there - John Barnes, Neil Ruddock and Rob Jones."

BELOW: Jamie Redknapp congratulated by his pals, Robbie Fowler and Steve McManaman after scoring in the Coca-Cola Cup against Burnley at Turf Moor.

# The Young Guns

## -ROBBIE FOWLER

Robbie Fowler started the season as a teenage sensation and the only thing that prevented him finishing as one was his 20th birthday last April.

He scored on the first day at Crystal Palace, then shot himself into the record books in Anfield's opening match with a hat-trick against Arsenal. It took only four minutes 38 seconds...the fastest hat-trick ever scored for Liverpool and the fastest in the short history of the Premier League.

Yet only a couple of years earlier, like the other Liverpool 17 year olds being put through their paces at the Nelwood training ground, he had looked enviously across at the big pitch, where all-time greats like Ian Rush and John Barnes were practising. And he wondered if he would ever join them.

Little did he know that from the age of 12 he had been picked out as a future star. No-one gets special treatment at Liverpool, so young Robbie was left to get on with it...and to dream. But not for long.

At 18 he was called up for a Coca-Cola Cup tie at Fulham and scored in a 3-1 win. Two weeks later the Reds won 5-0 at Anfield - and Robbie got all five.

Now the boy who once supported Everton was hailed as a great talent. The

The one that got away against Nottingham Forest.

Robbie Fowler salutes the final goal of his record-breaking hat-trick against Arsenal.

goals kept coming and so did the honours...England Youth and Under-21 caps, a call-up into the full England squad with Jamie Redknapp, and a new contract which binds him to Liverpool until 1998.

He has quite a collection of footballs he has claimed every time he scores a hat-trick, but despite his new-found fame, Robbie remains modest and keeps his feet on the ground. He explains, "How can I change with the coaching staff and senior players we have here? They wouldn't allow me if I wanted to." As for signing his new contract, he adds, "I love the place. I have no reason to to anywhere else."

Robbie also admits the debt he owes the great Ian Rush, who has been at his side during his amazing progress. "Ian has talked me through games and told me about the habits of opposing defenders. His goalscoring is second to none and he has won every prize in the game. I have been fortunate to play alongside him."

Robbie Fowler creates panic in the Sheffield Wedensday defence.

# The YOUNG GUNS

## -JAMIE REDKNAPP

Jamie Redknapp was born into the world of football and his journey to the top has been different to that of most young hopefuls who set out on the road to success.

As little more than a schoolboy he was transferred to Liverpool by his dad, Harry Redknapp, who was then manager of Bournemouth. Dad, a former wing star with West Ham, became manager at his old club and he and Jamie have found themselves on opposite sides in Premier League matches.

The tall, clean-cut midfielder became the youngest player in Liverpool history to appear in a European match when he was chosen against Auxerre of France in the UEFA cup at the age of 18 years and four months.

Injuries had meant he had to be thrown in at the deep end, so was life tough for a young man so far away from home? Jamie answers like a wise professional, "I come from a very close family, but I have also grown up with football and know the demands it makes."

That professionalism made Jamie a natural choice as captain of a highly successful England Under-21 team and earned him about 100 first-team appearances for Liverpool before his 21st birthday in June last year.

When Jamie, the team's pin-up, reported to Anfield for the new season it was to find sacks full of birthday cards waiting for him. He cuts a stylish figure on and off the field and admits that he has a weakness for designer suits and casual wear.

It was no surprise when he was presented last year with the trophy as the first-ever Player of the Year chosen by the

JAMIE REDKNAPP jumps for joy as his free kick flies into the Nottingham Forest net, then graciously credits it to Robbie Fowler who had deflected the ball in flight.

Liverpool International Supporters Club. He had an overwhelming majority of the votes.

Jamie's non-stop running and shooting power were rewarded in 1994 with a hat-trick for England Under-21 against Austria - and a new four-year contract with the Reds. The boy born to be a footballer responded with typical maturity, "I have been helped by older players and my turn is coming up to help the younger ones."

# The TOP GUN

Ian Rush entered 1995 still looking for new records to add to his goalscoring legend. His old playing partner, Kenny Dalglish, believes he has set the standards for all other strikers to aim at.

Dalglish, now manager of Blackburn Rovers, paid more than £8 million for his strike force, Alan Shearer and Chris Sutton, but they were outgunned when Ian destroyed Rovers in the Coca-Cola Cup last season with a devastating hat-trick.

Ian, still lean and hungry at the age of 33, was playing his 600th game for Liverpool and just a couple of weeks earlier he had achieved a century of goals in cup competition.

He is Liverpool's top scorer with well over 300 goals and also holds the record for Wales. He has winner's medals for League Championship, FA Cup, League Cup and European Cup.

Yet he remains modest about his success. In fact, as a teenager Ian thought he had achieved his big ambition when he joined his favourite football club, little Chester.

He was happy there as a young player, but soon big clubs, including

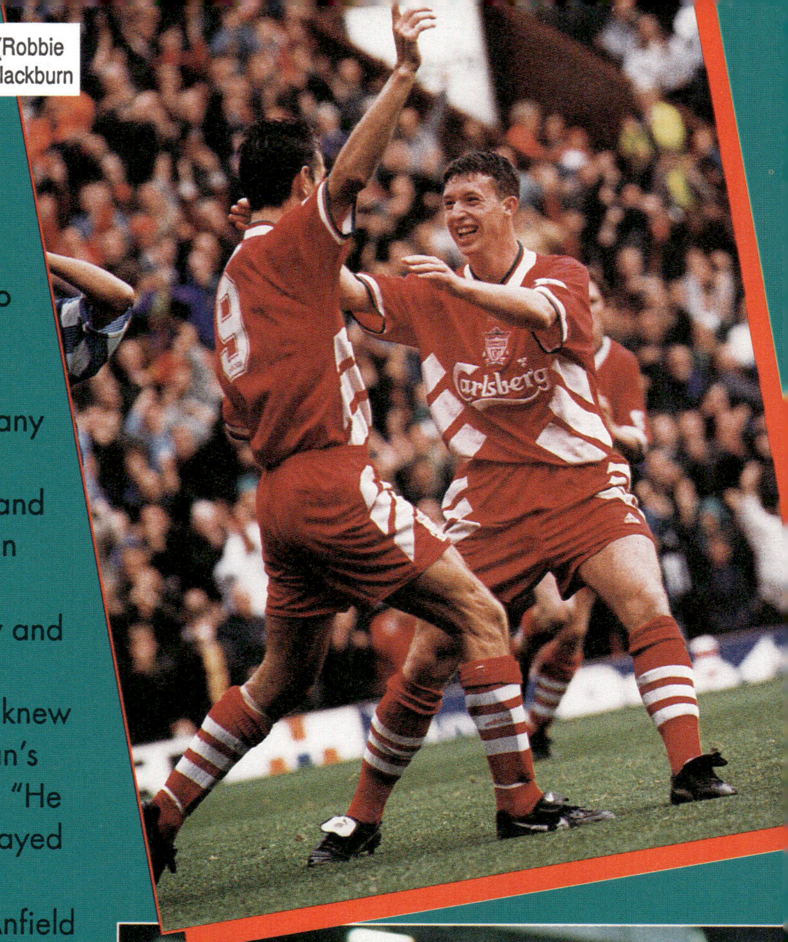

RIGHT: The Sorcerer (Ian Rush) and the apprentice (Robbie Fowler) in a magic moment during Ian's hat-trick at Blackburn

Liverpool, spotted his ability and tried to lure him away. Nowadays he tells the story of how he actually turned them down before manager Bob Paisley finally persuaded him to visit Anfield and become a Red.

"I didn't think I was good enough," says Ian. "They had so many top players there at the time."

The man who won everything and went on to become Liverpool captain started last season with a personal ambition - to receive a major trophy and hold it aloft in triumph.

His old captain, Alan Hansen, knew that feeling many times, thanks to Ian's goals. He says of the Welsh genius, "He is the best goalscorer I have ever played alongside or against."

Ian had one year away from Anfield with the famous Italian club Juventus. He flew home to play in Alan Hansen's testimonial match and recalls, "Whenever I went near the touchlines the fans kept asking, 'When are you coming back Rushie?'" So back he came.

Supporters showed their gratitude when Ian had his testimonial at the end of last year. More than 25,000 braved appalling weather and cheered their idol as he scored a typical goal in a 6-0 win against Celtic.

Ian in control watched by Sheffield Wednesday's John Sheridan

In the bag...star signings Phil Babb and John Scales

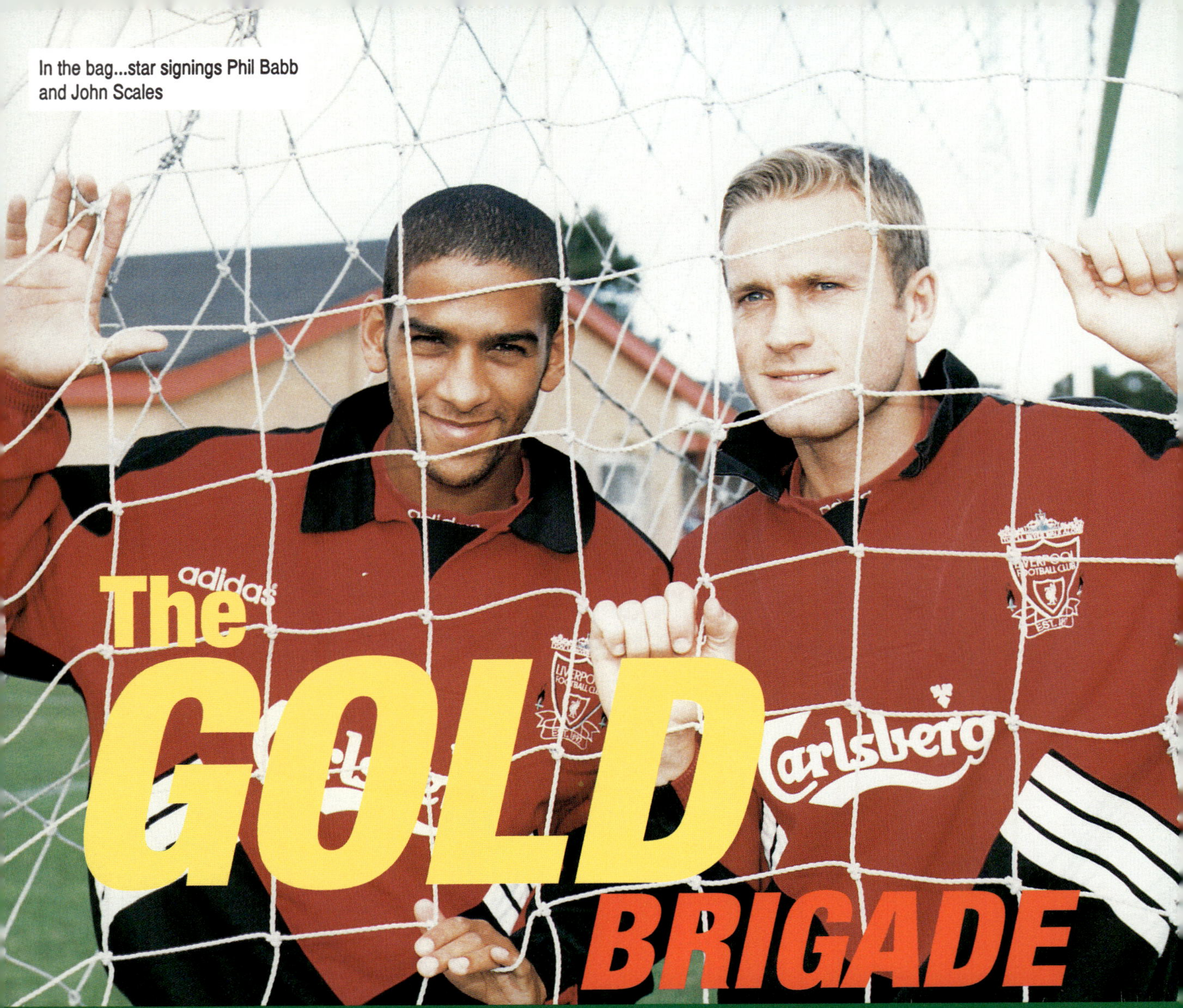


# The GOLD BRIGADE

John Scales completed a £9 million defensive wall when he signed for Liverpool with the season just three games old. He lined up alongside World Cup star Phil Babb, who had joined the club just 24 hours earlier, and Neil Ruddock, who had cost £2.5 million from Spurs the previous year.

The capture of Scales and Babb shook the football world and showed that Roy Evans had the money and the confidence to restore the Reds to greatness.

John fitted in immediately. "He looks as if he's played for Liverpool all his life," claimed the delighted manager as his calm, elegant centre-back slotted in to the right of Ruddock and won immediate acceptance from the Anfield crowd.

Many clubs had cast envious eyes at the tall, blond defender during his days at Wimbledon, where his class had stood out. Roy Evans had tried to sign him for a year without success because Wimbledon wanted a replacement before they would let John go.

When the chance finally came, John took just 15 minutes to make up his mind and announced, "I have joined one of the world's great clubs. It is a big opportunity for me, a chance to advance my football."

John is an outstanding example to all young players who suffer early disappointments and feel like giving up. He was rejected by Leeds United after joining them as a trainee 15 months earlier.

"That was a shock to the system and left me devastated," recalls John, a Yorkshireman

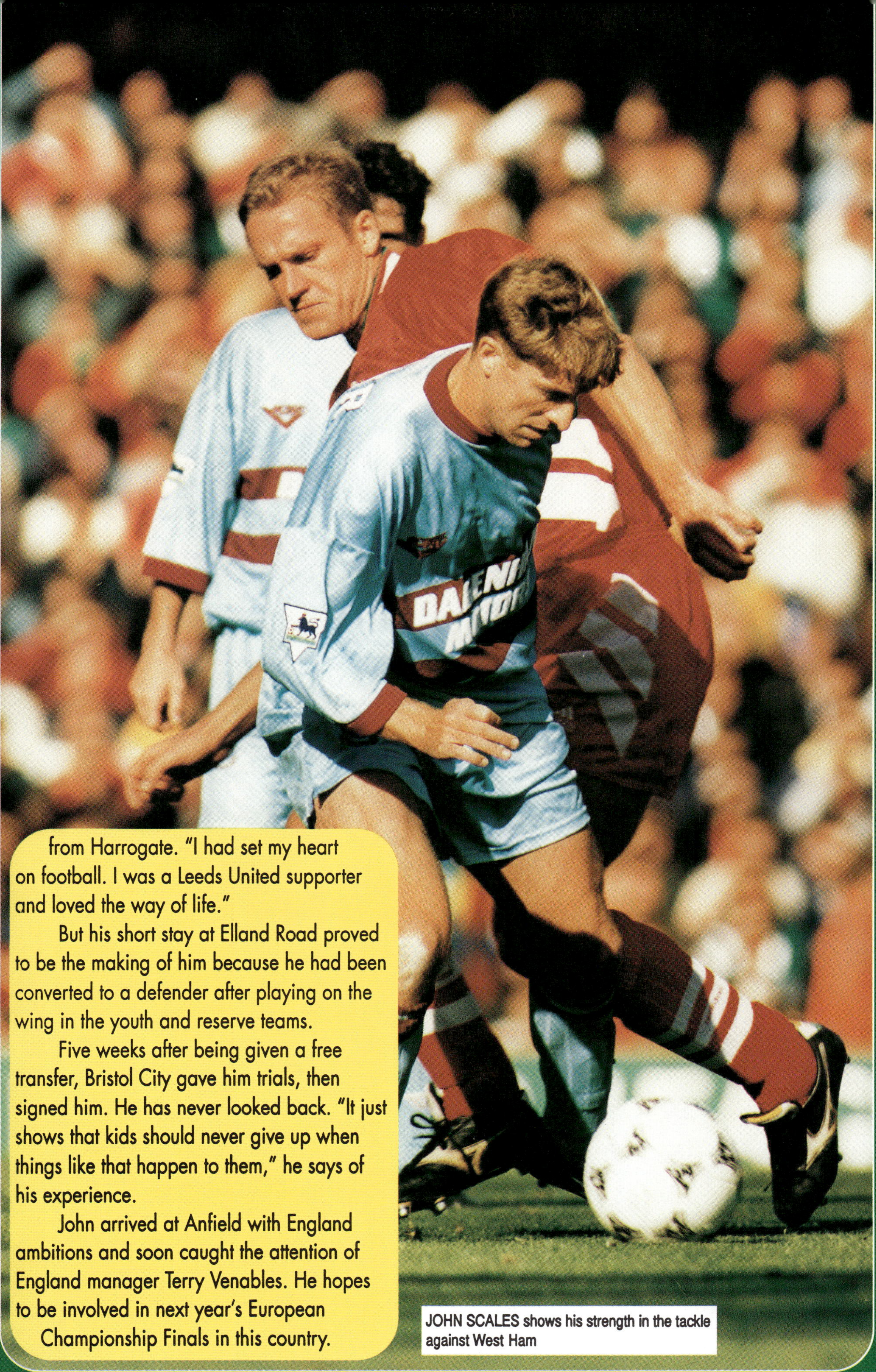

from Harrogate. "I had set my heart on football. I was a Leeds United supporter and loved the way of life."

But his short stay at Elland Road proved to be the making of him because he had been converted to a defender after playing on the wing in the youth and reserve teams.

Five weeks after being given a free transfer, Bristol City gave him trials, then signed him. He has never looked back. "It just shows that kids should never give up when things like that happen to them," he says of his experience.

John arrived at Anfield with England ambitions and soon caught the attention of England manager Terry Venables. He hopes to be involved in next year's European Championship Finals in this country.

JOHN SCALES shows his strength in the tackle against West Ham

There was a queue of clubs waiting to sign Phil Babb when he returned from the World Cup Final in America last year. And Liverpool were right at the front.

Television exposure had enhanced Phil's reputation as a highly promising defender with Coventry City, who had made him their captain at the age of 23.

In America he turned in outstanding performances for the Republic of Ireland, proving he was capable of man-marking some of the most talented attackers in the world.

Liverpool didn't need these star performances to confirm their judgement. They had watched Phil closely long before then, but had to be patient until Coventry could be persuaded to part with him.

Unlike John Scales, who followed him to Anfield 24 hours later, Phil took time to settle in. But once he had adapted to the new system of three central defenders, his speed and strength shone through.

His determination to succeed was never in doubt, for like John he had fought back after rejection early in his career. Phil had been given a free transfer while still a youngster with Millwall.

He had not set out on a soccer career. He was a student in Clapham when a Millwall scout saw him playing in a college game. After being offered trials, he was taken on as an apprentice.

Phil reflects, "I look back and feel fortunate that a scout happened to be there on that particular day and liked what he saw. I had not set my heart on a football career at

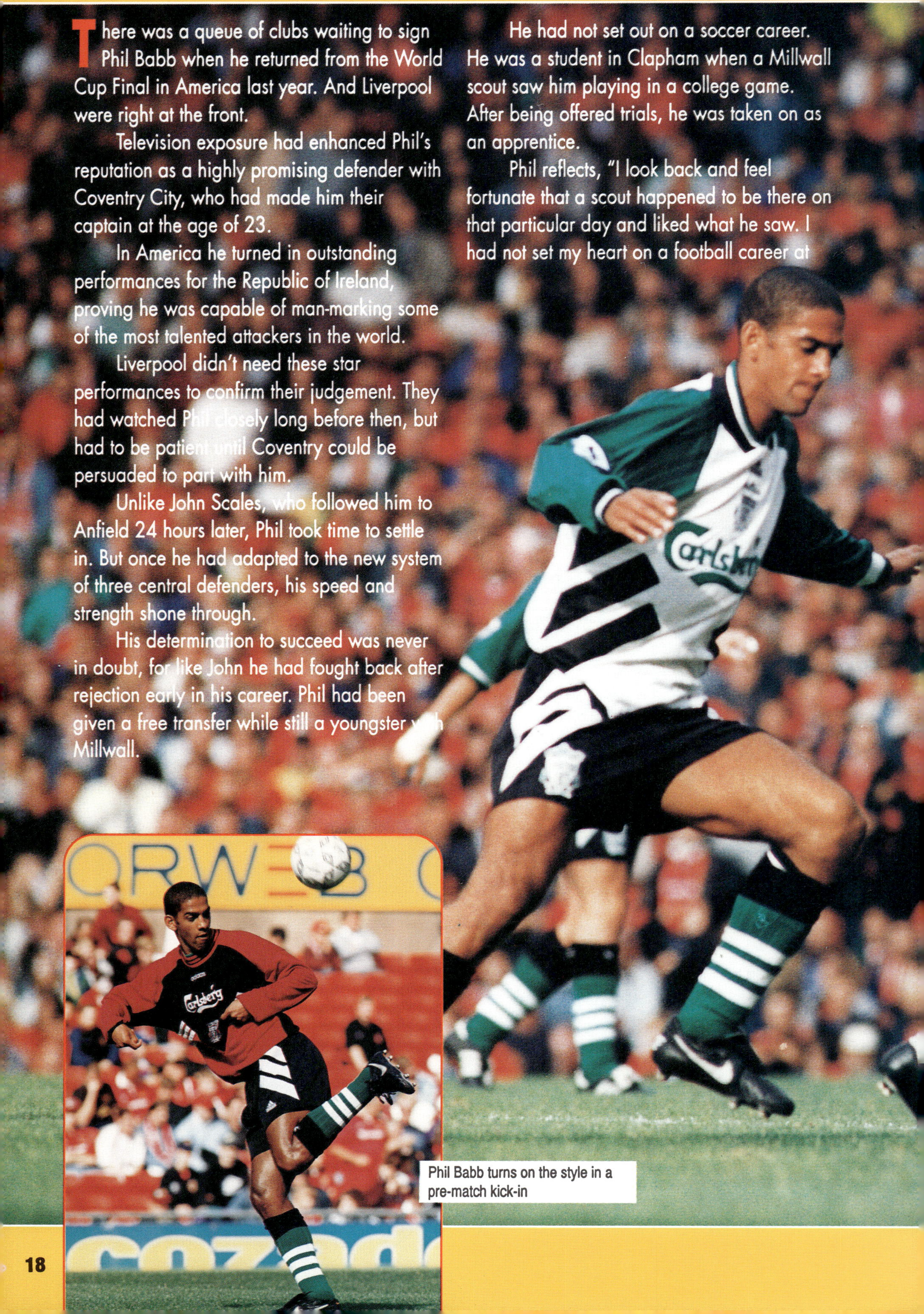

Phil Babb turns on the style in a pre-match kick-in

that time, in fact, I had not seen a game at any of the big grounds in London."

It took him only 48 hours to find a new club after Millwall. Bradford City took him on and he was soon attracting attention. Coventry stepped in with an offer which was accepted.

"The move was unexpected," says Phil. "But it was the start of the Premier League and I wanted to be competing with the best." So he joined manager Phil Neal, a former Liverpool captain, and has never looked back.

When he moved to Anfield one member of his family was particularly delighted - his nephew, Cameron, living in Lambeth and then aged four. Once he had finished signing and meeting the Press, Uncle Phil strolled over to the Souvenir Shop and bought him a new Liverpool strip.

Babb signs autographs for some appreciative fans

Tight marking by Phil Babb on Paul Ince of Manchester United

To the fans, who had no inkling that manager Roy Evans planned to block the road to Liverpool's goal with a golden wall of three top-priced central defenders, Neil Ruddock's future looked uncertain when Phil Babb and John Scales arrived.

Not any more. The big man, leaner and fitter than ever before, revelled in the challenge by producing the best form of his career. England recognition soon followed with a first cap against Nigeria in November last year.

Now he is an Anfield folk hero. Thousands of supporters love the 26 year old iron man for his enthusiasm, courage and commitment, but perhaps most of all because he obviously enjoys every moment he spends in a red shirt.

No catching Neil Ruddock after he blasted in a free kick against Aston Villa for his first goal of the season

He looks just as much at home in an England strip and showed at Wembley that apart from his acknowledged defensive strengths, he is a real problem when he goes forward for free-kicks and corners.

Neil has snatched vital goals, adding to the massive popularity he has attracted with his waves to the crowd, general good humour and the way he returns applause at the end of tough games.

The Londoner had played all his football in the South - with Millwall, Southampton and Spurs (twice) - before he found his true stage at Anfield. No-one there on the night of Liverpool's amazing fightback from 3-0 down to 3-3 against Manchester United in their double season will forget his headed equaliser.

But Neil couldn't remember it. He had been hurt in a clash of heads as he powered into the crowded goalmouth.

One of his biggest fans is former Liverpool and England goalkeeper Ray Clemence, once on the backroom staff at Spurs, who forecast soon after Neil's move to Liverpool that it would suit him perfectly and that his play would get better and better. Nobody at Anfield has ever disagreed with him.

Neil Ruddock wins the aerial battle at Blackburn

# THE REDS OF ENGLAND

Top of the heap... Regular internationals Rob Jones and John Barnes

Few players have hit the heights as quickly as Rob Jones. One day he was training with little Crewe Alexandra, then by the end of the week he was starring on television in his Liverpool debut at Old Trafford. The virtually unknown right-back, barely 20, kept Manchester United's wonderboy, Ryan Giggs, under control.

Five months later he was being hailed after another debut - for England against France at Wembley. Then to round the season off there was another great Wembley memory - an FA Cup winner's medal against Sunderland.

Rob's transfer to Liverpool in October, 1991 had been hurried through because the club were struggling with an injury crisis. The new boy followed the advice which all the coaches offer at Anfield, "When your first team chance comes along, grab it with both hands."

Rob has had to grab his chances twice, for that wonderful beginning with the club was followed by a season dogged by injury and illness. Since then he has gone from strength to strength and plays regularly for his country.

# Rob Jones

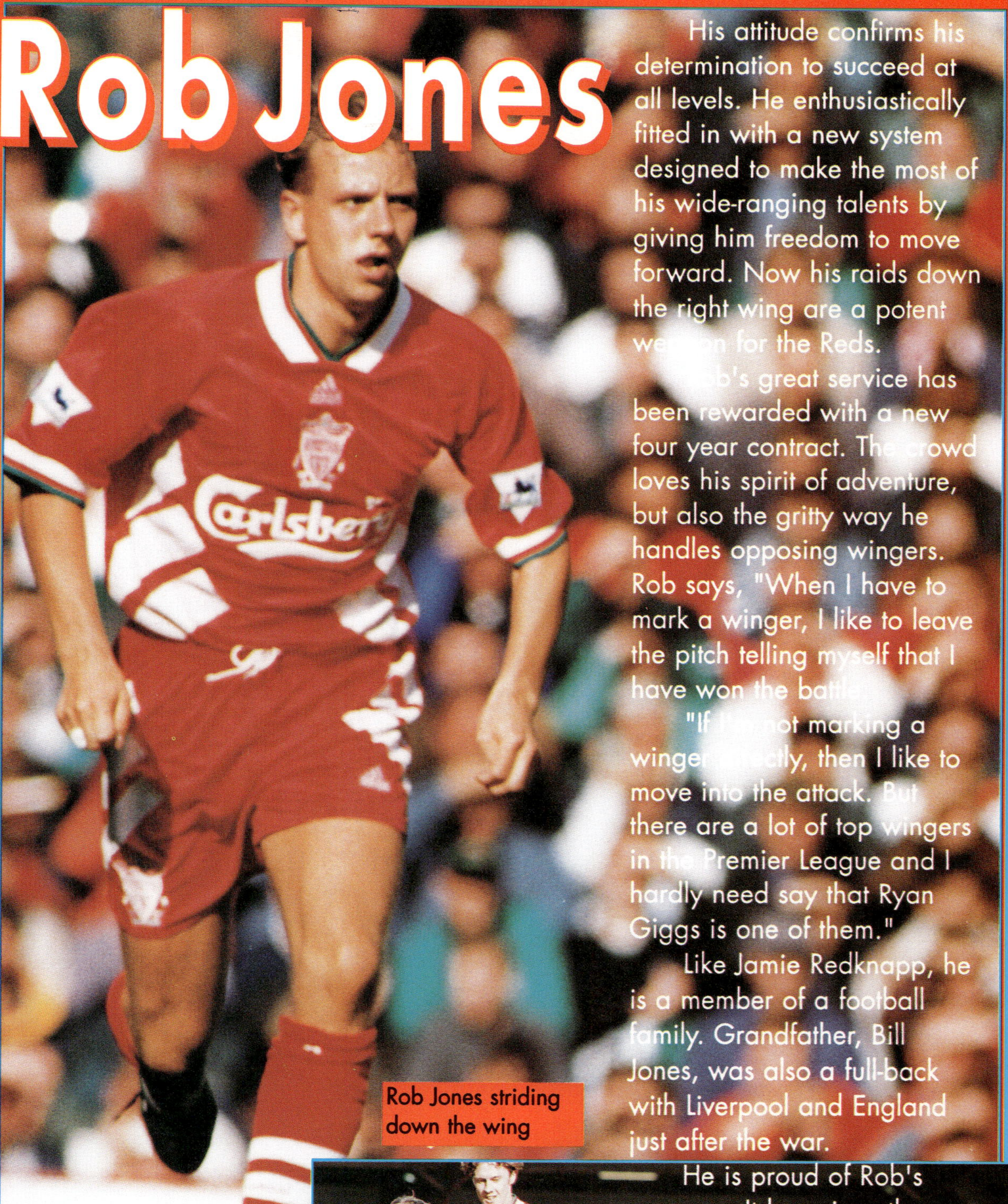

Rob Jones striding down the wing

His attitude confirms his determination to succeed at all levels. He enthusiastically fitted in with a new system designed to make the most of his wide-ranging talents by giving him freedom to move forward. Now his raids down the right wing are a potent weapon for the Reds.

Rob's great service has been rewarded with a new four year contract. The crowd loves his spirit of adventure, but also the gritty way he handles opposing wingers. Rob says, "When I have to mark a winger, I like to leave the pitch telling myself that I have won the battle.

"If I'm not marking a winger directly, then I like to move into the attack. But there are a lot of top wingers in the Premier League and I hardly need say that Ryan Giggs is one of them."

Like Jamie Redknapp, he is a member of a football family. Grandfather, Bill Jones, was also a full-back with Liverpool and England just after the war.

He is proud of Rob's progress. It has given the young star a maturity beyond his years and he feels at ease in the international gatherings. But he has his priorities in order and says, "If I am not playing well for my club, then I won't be picked for my country."

ROB JONES
BORN IN WREXHAM
5.11.71

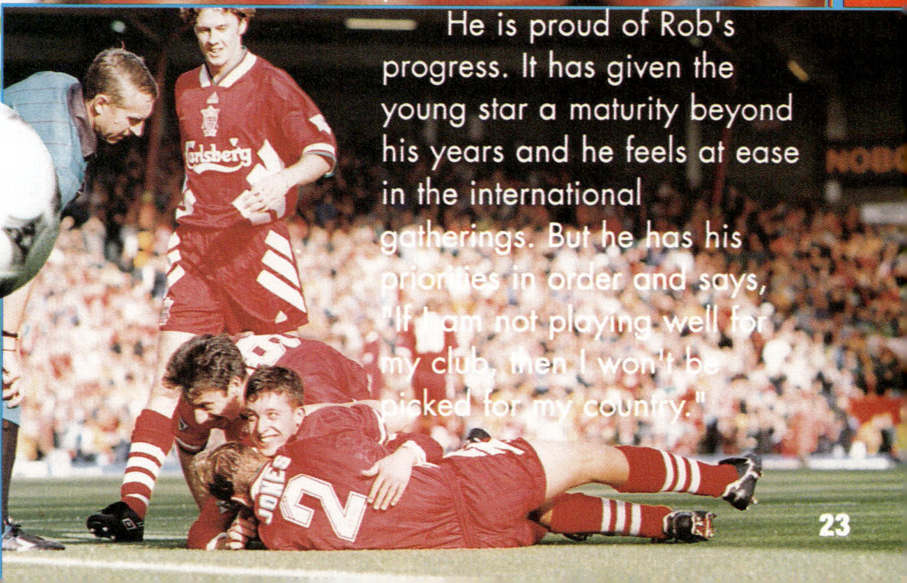

Bottom of the heap... Rob Jones after making the opening for a wonder goal by Robbie Fowler against Aston Villa

# John Barnes

Barnes in action

JOHN BARNES
BORN IN JAMAICA
7.11.63

No Liverpool player has won more England caps than John Barnes, but his international career seemed to be over once he had reached 33. The caps have been piling up again however, after a remarkable fightback.

For three seasons, John battled

against a run of achilles tendon and thigh problems. Every time he got close to full fitness, trouble would flare up again.

Throughout the summer of 1994, while team-mates relaxed, he worked alone, pounding country lanes near his home on three mile runs and sprinting up a nearby hill.

When the players reported for training that July, John was ready and razor sharp. He took on an attacking midfield role and the results of all that hard work were there to be seen as he twisted and turned past defenders, played superb passes and scored spectacular goals.

The new Barnes helped to restore the old Liverpool and people in football were full of praise for his dedication. But even he was surprised when Terry Venables called him up for England's first game of the season against the USA.

"I didn't think my chance would come so early," he says. "Not after so few games." He resisted the chance to hit back at critics who had begun to write him off and instead said simply, "I am back and playing regular football. That is the whole point."

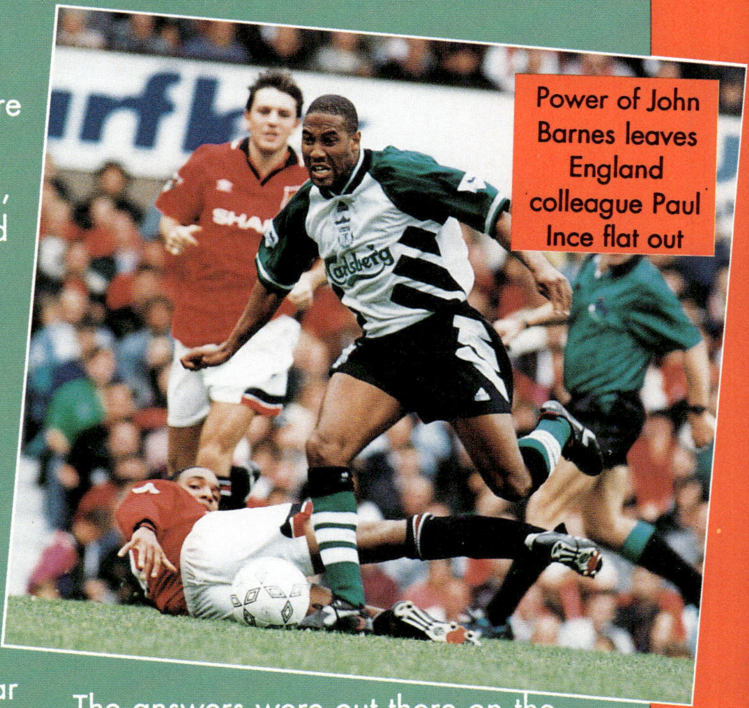

Power of John Barnes leaves England colleague Paul Ince flat out

The answers were out there on the pitch, where the young Reds benefited from his touch and wisdom. "I am pleased to be conditioned for 90 minutes of running up and down the field and doing the things I used to do," he says delightedly. "It was good to be back, trying to return Liverpool to the top, where they belong."

John made the best of his England comeback and his name joined that of Liverpool right-back Rob Jones on Terry Venables' list of first choices. They have fired the ambitions of a string of players at Anfield.

Balance of John Barnes and the flair, captured below with the overhead kick at Blackburn which was voted Goal of the month in BBC Match of the Day

Barnes overhead kick

# IN FROM THE COLD

Molby the playmaker... a master at work

JAN MOLBY
BORN IN KOLDING,
DENMARK 4.07.63

Jan Molby's prospects of an early comeback to the first team looked bleak with only two weeks to go to the season. He had suffered cruel luck with injuries and his fitness had not been put to the test after a calf operation two months earlier.

Perhaps if he'd been able to prove his strength and fitness on the tough pre-season tour...but he'd missed that. But while the burly Dane was preparing himself for a disappointment, his manager was thinking of Jan's legendary passing ability and deciding on a gamble.

He pitched Jan into the team for the opening game at Crystal Palace. The big man admits, "I did not expect to see my name on the team sheet, although every player likes to be in at the start."

He repaid the club by taking command of the game and launching the team towards a 6-1 victory with their first goal of the season, from the penalty spot. Jan recalls, "Players had a new spring in their step. I sensed that in the dressing room. We had something to prove."

He had not played in the first team since December 14, 1993, and had appeared in fewer than 30 games over the previous two seasons.

"It had been a very frustrating period of my life," says Jan. "There's no doubt that players value the game more when they've been out for a long spell."

The Reds were overjoyed to be able to call on his skill and defence-splitting talents again and prayed for a long run without interruptions by injury. Jan talked of his feelings, "I am trying to convert a weakness into a strength. I am thinking of all the pressure I have saved on my legs through missing so much football. "There is a lot of football left in me and I want to enjoy the future. I was 31 at the beginning of the season and I hope I'm still playing at the age of 35."

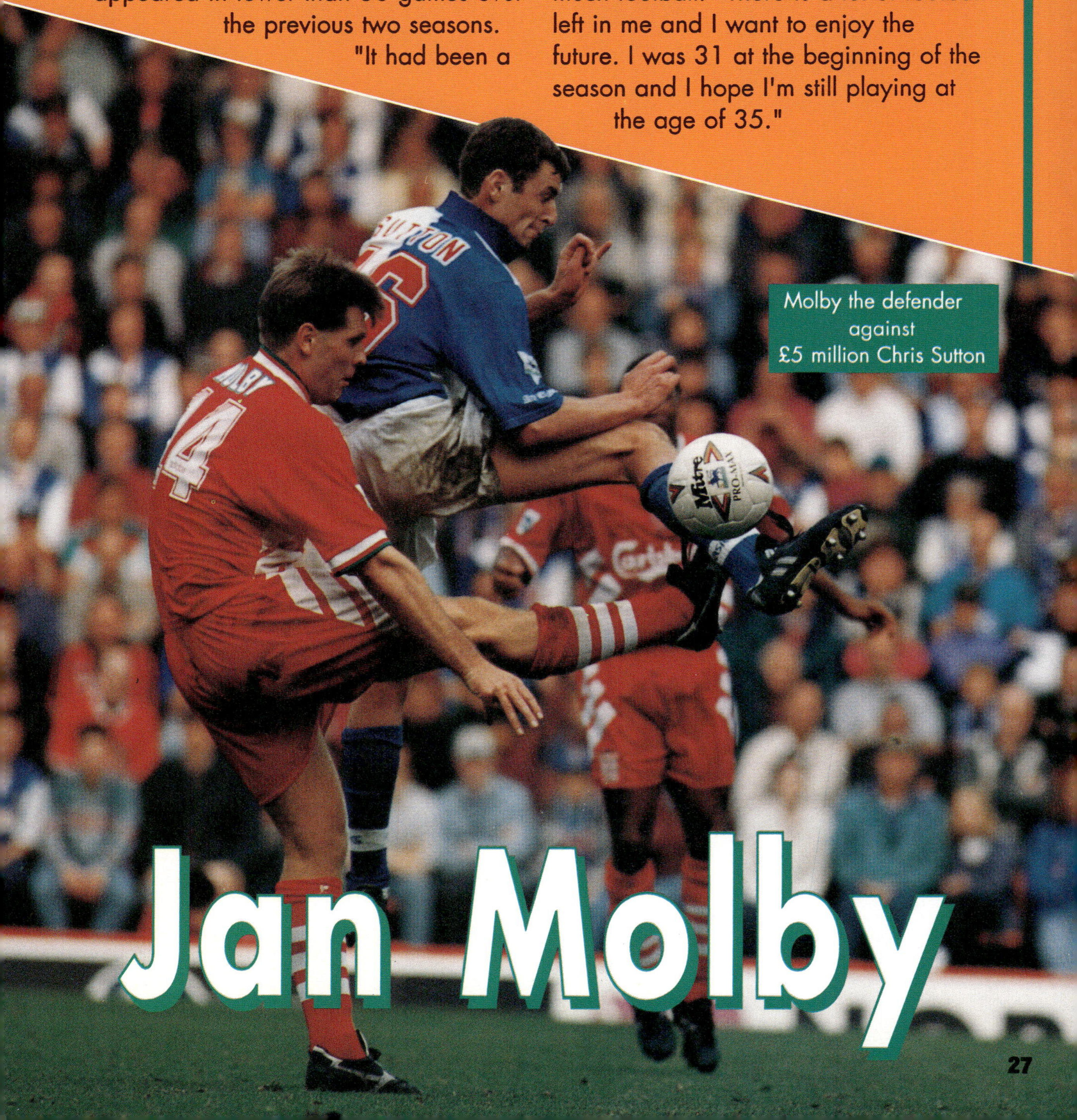


Molby the defender against £5 million Chris Sutton

# Jan Molby

# Stig Bjornebye

Stig on the attack

STIG BJORNEBYE
BORN IN ROSENBORG
11.12.69

Stig Bjornebye had to go back to Norway before he could feel thoroughly at home at Liverpool. Manager Roy Evans decided that's what was needed to build up the left-back's confidence.

Although he was a Norwegian international when Liverpool signed him from Rosenborg, Stig was short of experience as a full-time professional. He could not win a regular place at Anfield and this created worries that he might be left out of Norway's plans for the World Cup Finals.

Roy Evans thought carefully before agreeing to a temporary return to Rosenborg which would provide Stig with regular first-team football. A few weeks later, he went off to America with Norway and returned a new man.

Stig played against Mexico, Italy and the Republic of Ireland before his team were eliminated on goal difference. "It didn't last long, but it was valuable experience for me," he says. "Being on the same stage as so many great players did my confidence a lot of good."

He went back to Norway determined to make the grade with the Reds. Apart from a two week fishing break, he trained to keep himself in peak condition. "It was all worth while," he smiles. "I was ready for the new season's challenge when I reported back to Liverpool.

"Pre-season work is always hard,

Stig under attack...

but it didn't affect me nearly so much this time. I kept reminding myself that I had come to Liverpool to play first-team football."

His efforts were rewarded with instant selection and Stig's awareness and ability to move forward and hit deadly crosses with his left foot have become a feature of the team's play. He is also particularly dangerous with freekicks and corners.

Under the weather

# David James

DAVID JAMES
BORN IN WELWYN, HERTS.
1.08.70

David James is the son of an artist and loves to sketch caricatures of his team-mates

Goalkeeper David James was delighted to begin the season with his name on the Liverpool team sheet and a brand new No. 1 jersey on his dressing room peg. He had spent much of the previous two years waiting in the wings after his £1 million transfer from Watford.

Now he had a chance to leave the substitutes' bench for good. His old No.13 jersey was stowed away in a cupboard at home and he took his share of the credit as Liverpool's revival inspired praise.

But David thinks deeply about the game and is aware of the pitfalls. "If I don't put in the right performances, I might as well be No.13," he claims.

"People used to say that you were only as good as your last game, but that doesn't mean a lot today. You are only as good as the game you are playing. It is all down to the individual, not the number he wears."

The 6ft 5in young giant used his days on the first-team bench to study other goalkeepers in action and absorb the attacking methods of opposing teams so that he would know what to expect if called upon to face them.

He is ambitious and sets himself targets in his desire to improve. David explains, "As a youngster at Watford I would look at the number of clean sheets which keepers had kept before me. I would then try to beat them. I enjoyed the challenge."

Experts have noted that David has exceptional agility for such a big man and think that he has an international future with the right application. He was pleased when Liverpool appointed Joe Corrigan, ex-Manchester City and England, as goalkeeping coach during the season.

David enjoys the training and the discussions they share and says, "Joe played at the top level for a long time and I respect his thoughts and advice."

David points the way ahead

# IN THE WINGS

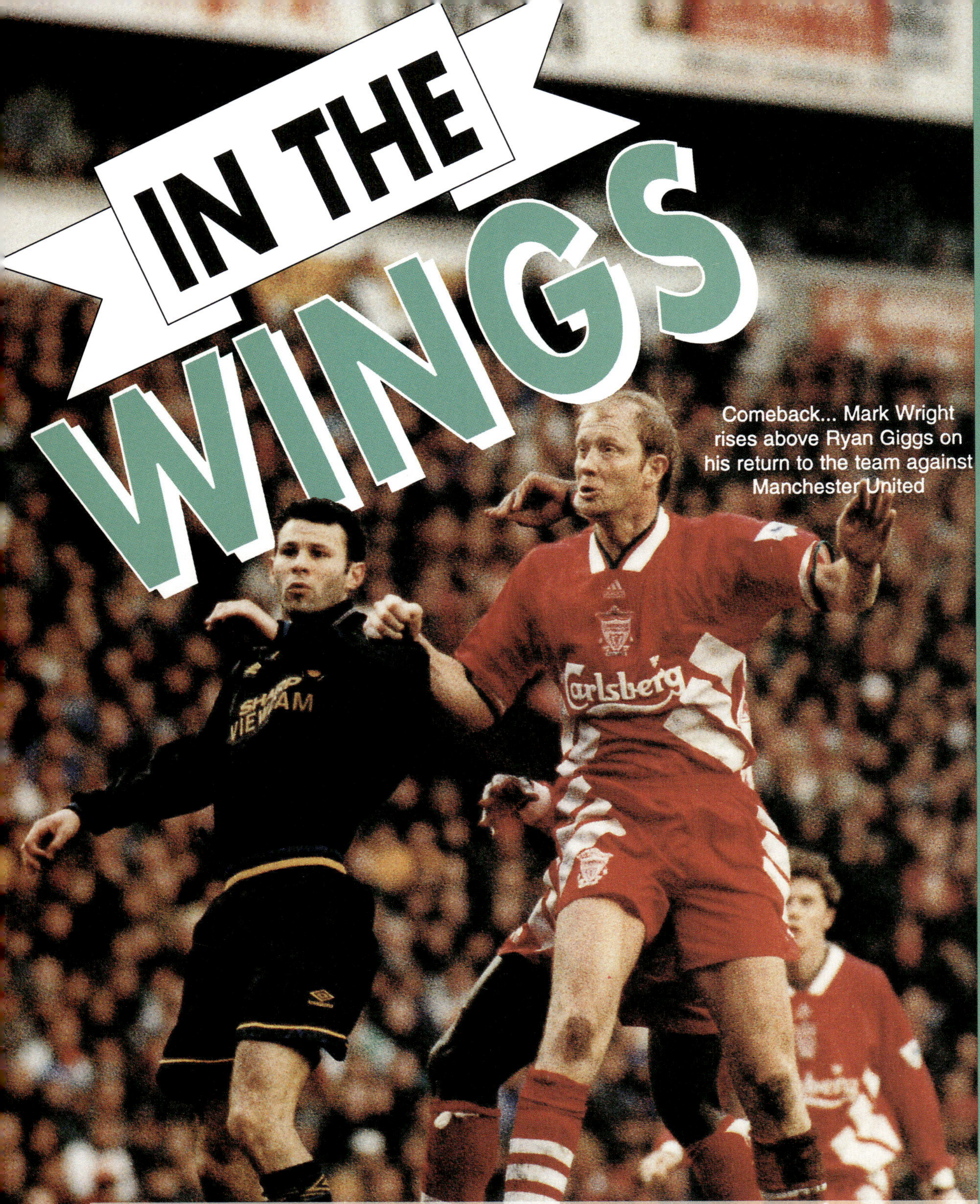


Comeback... Mark Wright rises above Ryan Giggs on his return to the team against Manchester United

Four England Internationals, who cost Liverpool a total of £7.5 million, had to sit out most of the season and the Coca-Cola Cup Final.

On the subs' bench at Wembley were former Arsenal midfielder Michael Thomas and winger Mark Walters, who followed former manager Graeme Souness from Rangers to Anfield.

Centre-back Mark Wright and striker Nigel Clough were there merely as spectators.

Nigel, who had left Nottingham Forest after the retirement of his father, Brian Clough, was a regular on the Liverpool bench up to Christmas, but was rarely called on.

His place in the team had gone to

Rob Jones, of England, chats to former internationals Mark Wright and Nigel Clough.

Robbie Fowler and there was no competing with a teenager described by his manager as, "the best young goalscorer I've ever seen."

Mark Walters spent weeks on loan with Wolves, helping them in the Division One promotion battle, but was welcomed back back by Roy Evans, subbed for Stig Bjornebye at Coventry on December 3 and remained a regular member of the squad.

A few weeks earlier, Michael Thomas, whose Liverpool career had been dogged by injuries, took over in the squad when Jan Molby, another regular casualty, broke down.

He was no stranger to Wembley, having scored a spectacular goal there in Liverpool's 2-0 FA Cup Final against Sunderland. Mark Wright was the Reds' skipper who held the trophy on high that day in 1992.

But he had been ruled out from the start of the 1994-95 season by injury and the success of new signings John Scales and Phil Babb, plus lack of match fitness, had made a return to the first team difficult.

His first-team comeback chance arrived on March 19 in the crunch game against Manchester United. Wright, who had not played in a serious first-team game for nearly a year, was outstanding.

Although he had to step down with the return of Rob Jones, he had proved that at 31, he was still a fine defender. He was given other chances to show it as the long, hard season took its toll in the closing weeks.

Team spirit was high as Liverpool spent a relaxing few hours at a parkland hotel before the final lap of the journey to Wembley. The men lucky enough to be chosen to play the Coca-Cola Cup Final received every encouragement from those destined to be mere spectators. In return they were offered sympathy and understanding to help them get over their disappointment.

Midfield general John Barnes is pictured on a stroll with substitutes Michael Thomas and Mark Walters.

# HIGHLIGHTS Of A Season

Even Liverpool's most ardent supporters could not believe their team's stunning start to the season that was to produce a record-breaking fifth League Cup (this one sponsored by Coca-Cola) and a place in Europe.

Their summer build-up had hardly been impressive, although Robbie Fowler managed nine goals in pre-season games and manager Roy Evans claimed to have learned valuable lessons from experiments with his team.

One was the need for Jan Molby's passing ability. The big Dane, still recovering from a knee operation and eight months out of action, was the surprise name in the Liverpool line-up for the opening game at Crystal Palace.

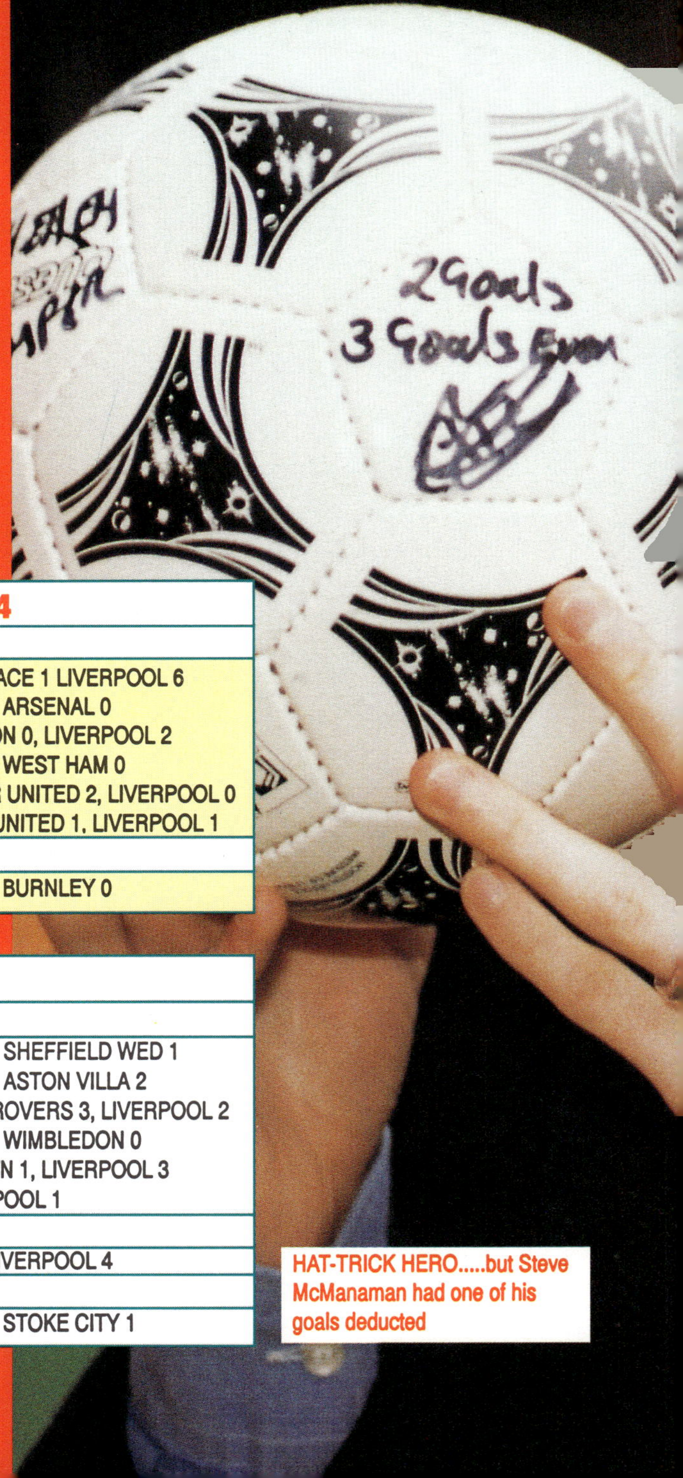

HAT-TRICK HERO.....but Steve McManaman had one of his goals deducted

**MATCH FAX...AUGUST/SEPTEMBER 1994**

| | | | |
|---|---|---|---|
| **PREMIERSHIP** | | | |
| 20.8.94 | Selhurst Park | Att: 18,084 | CRYSTAL PALACE 1 LIVERPOOL 6 |
| 28.8.94 | Anfield | Att: 30,017 | LIVERPOOL 3, ARSENAL 0 |
| 31.8.94 | The Dell | Att: 15,190 | SOUTHAMPTON 0, LIVERPOOL 2 |
| 10.9.94 | Anfield | Att: 30,907 | LIVERPOOL 0, WEST HAM 0 |
| 17.9.94 | Old Trafford | Att: 43,740 | MANCHESTER UNITED 2, LIVERPOOL 0 |
| 24.9.94 | St James' | Att: 34,435 | NEWCASTLE UNITED 1, LIVERPOOL 1 |
| **COCA-COLA CUP ROUND TWO, FIRST LEG** | | | |
| 21.9.94 | Anfield | Att: 23,359 | LIVERPOOL 2, BURNLEY 0 |

**MATCH FAX...OCTOBER 1994**

| | | | |
|---|---|---|---|
| **PREMIERSHIP** | | | |
| 1.10.94 | Anfield | Att: 31,493 | LIVERPOOL 4, SHEFFIELD WED 1 |
| 8.10.94 | Anfield | Att: 32,158 | LIVERPOOL 3, ASTON VILLA 2 |
| 15.10.94 | Ewood Park | Att: 30,263 | BLACKBURN ROVERS 3, LIVERPOOL 2 |
| 22.10.94 | Anfield | Att: 31,139 | LIVERPOOL 3, WIMBLEDON 0 |
| 29.10.94 | Portman Road | Att: 22,513 | IPSWICH TOWN 1, LIVERPOOL 3 |
| 31.10.94 | Loftus Road | Att: 18,295 | QRP 2, LIVERPOOL 1 |
| **COCA-COLA CUP SECOND ROUND, SECOND LEG** | | | |
| 5.10.94 | Turf Moor | Att: 19,032 | BURNLEY 1, LIVERPOOL 4 |
| **COCA-COLA CUP THIRD ROUND** | | | |
| 25.10.94 | Anfield | Att: 32,060 | LIVERPOOL 2, STOKE CITY 1 |

BIG DEAL.....Phil Babb welcomed to Anfield by manager Roy Evans

HAT-TRICK HERO..Ian Rush completes his one-man destruction of Blackburn Rover.

## MATCH FAX........NOVEMBER 1994

| | | | |
|---|---|---|---|
| **PREMIERSHIP** | | | |
| 5.11.94 | Anfield | Att: 33,329 | LIVERPOOL 1 NOTTINGHAM FOREST 0 |
| 9.11.95 | Anfield | Att: 32,855 | LIVERPOOL 3 CHELSEA 1 |
| 21.11.94 | Goodison Park | Att: 39,866 | EVERTON 2 LIVERPOOL 0 |
| 26.11.94 | Anfield | Att: 35,007 | LIVERPOOL 1 SPURS 1 |
| **COCA-COLA CUP FOURTH ROUND** | | | |
| 30.11.94 | Ewood Park | Att: 30,115 | BLACKBURN ROVERS 1 LIVERPOOL 3 |

Jan's penalty goal early in the game and the brilliance of Steve McManaman - to be repeated throughout the season, especially on an April day at Wembley - laid the foundations for a 6-1 win. Steve's two goals against Palace ended a 12-month blank spell and gave him the confidence to torment other teams with his free-to-roam role.

The Ian Rush-Robbie Fowler combination were also on the scoresheet. Eight days later Robbie took Anfield and Arsenal by storm in the first game in front of the half-finished new Kop Grandstand.

His breathtaking finishing was rewarded with three goals in 4 minutes 33 seconds - the fastest hat-trick in Liverpool history. Three days after that, the 19-year-old struck his fifth goal in three games, beating Bruce Grobbelaar, who was facing his old club for the first time after joining Southampton in the close season.

John Barnes, already showing enough class in his new midfield guise to retain the faith of England manager Terry Venables, got the other goal in a convincing 2-0 win at The Dell.

Excitement on Merseyside reached fever pitch a few days later when Roy Evans, after a fruitless summer in search of a big signing, captured Wimbledon's John Scales and Coventry's Phil Babb at a cost of more than £6million. Scales made his debut immediately against West Ham, with Babb on the subs' bench.

There was a feeling of anti-climax when the Hammers held out for a goalless draw and

## MATCH FAX...DECEMBER 1994

**PREMIERSHIP**

| | | | |
|---|---|---|---|
| 3.12.94 | Highfield Road | Att: 21,029 | COVENTRY CITY 1 LIVERPOOL 1 |
| 11.12.94 | Anfield | Att: 30,972 | LIVERPOOL 0 CRYSTAL PALACE 0 |
| 18.12.94 | Stamford Bridge | Att: 27,050 | CHELSEA 0 LIVERPOOL 1 |
| 26.12.94 | Filbert Street | Att: 21,393 | LEICESTER CITY 1 LIVERPOOL 1 |
| 28.12.94 | Anfield | Att: 38,122 | LIVERPOOL 2 MANCHESTER CITY 0 |
| 31.12.94 | Elland Road | Att: 38,563 | LEEDS UNITED 0 LIVERPOOL 2 |

uncertainty set in when the Reds went on to lose 2-0 at Old Trafford, despite outshining the Champions. Babb came on for the last 20 minutes, but when the Reds ended September by taking their first step on the road to Wembley, he was back on the bench.

John Scales, however, was out there on the pitch against First Division Burnley and heading Liverpool into the lead in the Coca-Cola Cup campaign. Six minutes from the end a shot of Fowler genius gave them a respectable 2-0 lead to take to Turf Moor for the second leg of the second-round tie.

Two weeks later, he scored against Burnley again, with Jamie Redknapp getting two and Nigel Clough the other in a comfortable 4-1 win. In between the Cup games, the Reds had turned on the style at Newcastle and at home to Sheffield Wednesday.

Terry Venables was at Newcastle as the Reds became the first team to take a point out of Kevin Keegan's men. He noted the form of Neil Ruddock and McManaman and both were later called up for England.

Against Wednesday 'Macca' claimed a hat-trick in a 4-1 victory and got to keep the match ball, although one of his strikes was later credited as an own goal.

Another home victory followed against Aston Villa, then it was confrontation time at Blackburn against the title-hungry Rovers managed by former Anfield idol Kenny

SCORER..John Scales signals his first Premiership goal for the Reds to the delight of teammates John Barnes and Neil Ruddock.

## MATCH FAX...JANUARY 1995

| | | | |
|---|---|---|---|
| **Premiership** | | | |
| 2.1.95 | Anfield | Att: 34,709 | LIVERPOOL 4 NORWICH CITY 0 |
| 14.1.95 | Anfield | Att: 32,733 | LIVERPOOL 0 IPSWICH TOWN 1 |
| 24.1.95 | Anfield | Att: 39,505 | LIVERPOOL 0 EVERTON 0 |
| **FA Cup Third Round** | | | |
| 7.1.95 | St Andrews | Att: 25,326 | BIRMINGHAM CITY 0 LIVERPOOL 0 |
| **FA Cup Third Round Replay** | | | |
| 18.1.95 | Anfield | Att: 36,275 | LIVERPOOL 1 BIRMINGHAM CITY 1 (Liverpool win penalty shoot-out 2-0) |
| **FA Cup Fourth Round** | | | |
| 28.1.95 | Turf Moor | Att: 20,551 | BURNLEY 0 LIVERPOOL 0 |
| **Coca-Cola Cup Fifth Round** | | | |
| 11.1.95 | Anfield | Att: 36,004 | LIVERPOOL 1 ARSENAL 0 |

Dalglish. Liverpool were outstanding and John Barnes scored with an overhead kick that was voted Match of the Day's Goal of the Month.

Robbie Fowler had opened the scoring. But the new-look, three man central defence of Scales, Ruddock and Babb proved vulnerable against the SAS - Rovers' mega-priced strikers Sutton and Shearer. The Reds lost 3-2.

Consolation came in the shape of a 3-0 win over their bogey team, Wimbledon, after nine unsuccessful attempts to beat them. Steve McManaman scored an exquisite first goal, then Robbie Fowler and John Barnes joined in.

Three days later the Reds celebrated a 2-1 Coco-Cola Cup win over third-round opponents Stoke City and a century of Cup goals for Ian Rush, who got two on the night. But the draw for the next round looked ominous...Blackburn at Ewood Park on November 30.

The Reds started November with home wins against Nottingham Forest and Chelsea, but their morale was put to the test in the Mersey derby match at Goodison, where struggling Everton powered their way to 2-0 in a memorable opening match for manager Joe Royle. Then Spurs were presented with a 1-1 draw at Anfield by a Neil Ruddock own goal.

A magic spark was needed at Blackburn - and Ian Rush provided it. The veteran striker scored a brilliant hat-trick, the Reds won 3-1 and Roy Evans declared, "Rushie is different class." Opposing manager Dalglish, his old

RIGHT: THE GOAL THAT BOOKED A TRIP TO WEMBLEY... Robbie Fowler shoots past Nigel Martyn.

BELOW: QUICK CHANGE...After scoring against Newcastle Robbie Fowler got round the F.A.'s ban on removing shirts by turning his back-to-front. Neil Ruddock saw the funny side.

## MATCH FAX...FEBRUARY/MARCH 1995

| | | | |
|---|---|---|---|
| **Premiership** | | | |
| 4.2.95 | City Ground | Att: 25,418 | NOTTINGHAM FOREST 1 LIVERPOOL 1 |
| 11.2.95 | Anfield | Att: 35,996 | LIVERPOOL 1 QPR 1 |
| 25.2.95 | Hillsborough | Att: 31,964 | SHEFFIELD WED 1 LIVERPOOL 2 |
| 4.3.95 | Anfield | Att: 39,300 | LIVERPOOL 2 NEWCASTLE UNITED 0 |
| 14.3.95 | Anfield | Att: 27,183 | LIVERPOOL 2 COVENTRY CITY 3 |
| 19.3.95 | Anfield | Att: 38,906 | LIVERPOOL 2 MANCHESTER UNITED 0 |
| 22.3.95 | White Hart Lane | Att: 31,988 | SPURS 0 LIVERPOOL 0 |
| **FA Cup Fourth Round Replay** | | | |
| 7.2.95 | Anfield | Att: 32,109 | LIVERPOOL 1 BURNLEY 0 |
| **FA Cup Fifth Round** | | | |
| 19.2.95 | Anfield | Att: 25,124 | LIVERPOOL 1 WIMBLEDON 1 |
| **FA Cup Fifth Round Replay** | | | |
| 28.2.95 | Selhurst Park | Att: 12,553 | WIMBLEDON 0 LIVERPOOL 2 |
| **FA Cup Sixth Round** | | | |
| 11.3.95 | Anfield | Att: 39,592 | LIVERPOOL 1 SPURS 2 |
| **Coca-Cola Semi-Final, First Leg** | | | |
| 15.2.95 | Anfield | Att: 25,480 | LIVERPOOL 1 CRYSTAL PALACE 0 |
| **Coca-Cola Semi-Final, Second Leg** | | | |
| 8.3.95 | Selhurst Park | Att: 18,224 | CRYSTAL PALACE 0 LIVERPOOL 1 |

Steve McManaman in typical devastating style

striking partner, added, "Ian Rush is a magnificent asset to Liverpool Football Club."

Gloom returned, however, as the Reds failed to win at Coventry and Chelsea and at home to Crystal Palace. In all, their last five Premiership games had yielded only four points and the Championship pacesetters, Blackburn and Machester United, had opened up quite a gap.

Christmas had a treat in store. A maximum 12 points were extracted from the bank holiday games at Leicester and Leeds and at Anfield against Manchester City and Norwich. Robbie had got five of the holiday goals, Ian Rush a couple and even the cautious Roy Evans was saying, "We could be in with a title shout."

But in January there were Cup battles to be fought. Liverpool had not won an FA Cup tie since the 1992 Final against Sunderland. In

1993 they had gone out of Bolton in the third round after a replay and suffered a similar fate against Bristol City in 1994. This time the B line led them to Birmingham, where the tie ended 0-0.

Would the jinx strike again? The answer to that question had to wait until after the crucial visit of Arsenal in the quarter-finals of the Coco-Cola Cup. John Barnes worked a cunning free-kick with Ian Rush, who pounced to snatch the only goal. It took his League Cup total to 48...just two short of the record set by England's 1966 World Cup hero Geoff Hurst.

Three days later, struggling Ipswich Town achieved their first-ever win at Anfield, then Birmingham arrived to force a 1-1 draw. It took a dramatic penalty shoot-out to remove them from the FA Cup. The jinx was over, but the Reds were in the middle of a goals drought.

DOUBLE WINNER..The man who took over the Coca Cola Cup Final .

They scored only six in 11 games after their 4-0 defeat of Norwich on January 2. Four of these were in Cup competitions and each one proved to be precious. In the FA Cup Jamie Redknapp's vital goal against Birmingham was followed by a John Barnes headed winner in a fourth-round replay against Burnley, who came closer to beating the Reds than they had in the Coco-Cola Cup.

Robbie Fowler snatched the others, starting with Crystal Palace in the first leg of the Coco-Cola semi-final at Anfield on February 15. Palace's tightened-up defence held out until the final seconds of injury time, then Robbie pounced to snatch the advantage away from them.

Four days later his first-ever FA Cup goal, wiped out an early lead taken by fifth-round opponents Wimbledon, who left Anfield happy with a 1-1 draw. Still, the month ended on a high note for the Reds...a 2-1 win at Hillsborough put them back on course in the Premiership, then John Barnes and Ian Rush crushed the Dons in the FA Cup replay to confirm that their hold over Liverpool had been broken.

John headed the first, then his inspired pass opened up the way for Ian to make history with a brilliant second. It was the master marksman's 41st FA Cup goal, equalling the great Denis Law's record.

But Ian was destined to pass neither him nor Geoff Hurst in the remaining Cup games.

A Rush-Fowler 2-0 win over Newcastle set the Liverpool mood for the Coca-Cola Cup semi-final return to Selhurst Park, where they triumphed by a single goal after a shaky start. Robbie opened the gates of Wembley with an ice-cool finish that let goalkeeper Nigel Marytn helpless, but Steve McManaman was the Coca-Cola Man of the Match.

Three days later they were back on the Wembley trail, facing Spurs at Anfield in the FA Cup quarter-finals and theoretically the only team in the country still with a chance of all three major trophies. Robbie headed them into the lead, but England's Terry Sheringham and Germany's Jurgen Klinsmann hit back as the

MAC MAGIC...He squeezes the ball past Keith Branagan for Liverpool's first goal, the calmly curls a shot just inside the post for the decider

weary Reds ran out of steam.

Within 72 hours they were losing at home to Coventry City, but made a dramatic improvement against Manchester United, whose efforts to retain the Championship were severely dented by a convincing 2-0 defeat. Jamie Redknapp, England Under-21 skipper, had the game of his life, scored a goal and earned a first call-up for the full England squad.

There was news in the transfer market, too. Roy Evans pulled off another big deal, paying Millwall £2 million for young Irishman Mark Kennedy, a lifelong Liverpool fan, to make him the dearest 18-year-old signing in British soccer history.

His arrival came at an exciting time. Although there could be no letting-up in the battle to finish as high as possible in the Premiership, all thoughts were now focused on their only chance to finish the season with a trophy...the Coca-Cola Cup Final on April 2.

The Reds knew that Bolton Wanderers, from the Endsleigh League First Division, would be worthy opponents. Wanderers, great cupfighters, had a collection of famous scalps, including Liverpool's when they were FA Cup holders.

Young Steve McManaman had helped win that FA Cup in 1992. Now, in 1995, he was shaking the hand of the legendary Sir Stanley Matthews as the teams lined up at Wembley. And he was about to have a final named after him, just as Sir Stanley did with Blackpool in 1953.

The old Wizard of Dribble looked on

IT'S OURS...Captain Ian Rush holds the Coca Cola Cup aloft.

## MATCH FAX...APRIL/MAY 1995

| | | | |
|---|---|---|---|
| **COCA-COLA FINAL CUP FINAL** | | | |
| 2.4.95 | Wembley | Att: 75,595 | BOLTON WANDERERS 1 LIVERPOOL 2 |
| **PREMIERSHIP** | | | |
| 5.4.95 | Anfield | Att: 29,881 | LIVERPOOL 3 SOUTHAMPTON 1 |
| 9.4.95 | Anfield | Att: 37,454 | LIVERPOOL 0 LEEDS UNITED 1 |
| 12.4.95 | Highbury | Att: 38,036 | ARSENAL 0 LIVERPOOL 1 |
| 14.4.95 | Maine Road | Att: 27,055 | MANCHESTER CITY 2 LIVERPOOL 1 |
| 17.4.95 | Anfield | Att: 36,012 | LIVERPOOL 2 LEICESTER CITY 0 |
| 29.4.95 | Carrow Road | Att: 21,843 | NORWICH CITY 1 LIVERPOOL 2 |
| 2.5.95 | Selhurst Park | Att: 12,041 | WIMBLEDON 0 LIVERPOOL 0 |
| 6.5.95 | Villa Park | Att: 40,154 | ASTON VILLA 2 LIVERPOOL 0 |
| 10.5.95 | Upton Park | Att: 22,446 | WEST HAM 3 LIVERPOOL 0 |
| 13.5.95 | Anfield | Att: 40,014 | LIVERPOOL 2 BLACKBURN ROVERS 1 |

approvingly as 'Macca' ran Bolton dizzy. In the 39th minute he scored a memorable goal, beating Alan Stubbs and Scott Green in a diagonal run before shooting past Keith Branagan. His second, after 67 minutes, was even better.

There seemed to be no danger when he collected the ball on the left touchline, but he cut in past Green and Mark Seagrave before calmly bending a shot just inside the post. Alan Thompson, who brought a breathtaking save from David James early in the game, volleyed a fine goal for Wanderers, but Liverpool finished deserving winners.

The much-decorated Ian Rush achieved his greatest remaining ambition - to collect a trophy as skipper of the Reds and hold it proudly above his head. He had become the League Cup's only five time winner.

'Macca' also collected the Alan Hardaker Trophy as the Man of the Final plus treasured words of praise from Sir Stanley, who made the presentations. Looking on with pride as the trophies were paraded before their joyful followers was Roy Evans, the one-time Bill Shankly apprentice who, 30 years later, had taken his place in the line of successful Liverpool managers.

Seven days after The McManaman Final another piece of silverware was added to the season's haul. Goalscoring prodigy Robbie Fowler said goodbye to teenage and received a very special 20th birthday present - the Professional Footballers Association Young Player of the Year Award.

The rewards continued to pile up. Robbie, John Scales and David james received their first invitations to join the full England party for a weekend get together. Pride had been restored to Anfield.

# LIVERPOOL'S ROLL OF HONOUR

| Competition | Times | Dates |
|---|---|---|
| LEAGUE CHAMPIONS | 18 | 1900-01, 1905-06, 1921-22, 1922-23, 1946-47, 1963-64, 1965-66, 1972-73, 1975-76, 1976-77, 1978-79, 1979-80, 1981-82, 1982-83, 1983-84, 1985-86, 1987-88, 1989-90 |
| PREMIER LEAGUE CHAMPIONS | 0 | |
| CHAMPIONSHIP RUNNERS-UP | 10 | 1898-99, 1909-10, 1968-69, 1973-74 1974-75, 1977-78, 1984-85, 1986-87 1988-89, 1990-91 0 |
| SECOND DIVISION CHAMPIONS | 3 | 1893-94, 1904-05, 1961-62 |
| SECOND DIVISION RUNNERS-UP | 0 | |
| FA CUP WINNERS | 5 | 1965, 1974, 1986, 1989, 1992 |
| FA CUP RUNNERS-UP | 5 | 1914, 1950, 1971, 1977, 1988 |
| LEAGUE CUP WINNERS | 5 | 1981, 1982, 1983, 1984, 1995 |
| LEAGUE CUP RUNNERS-UP | 2 | 1978, 1987 |
| EUROPEAN CUP WINNERS | 4 | 1977, 1978, 1981, 1984 |
| EUROPEAN CUP RUNNERS-UP | 1 | 1985 |
| UEFA CUP WINNERS | 2 | 1973, 1976 |
| EUROPEAN CWC RUNNERS-UP | 1 | 1966 |

LIVERPOOL
LIVERPOOL
LIVERPOOL F.C
LIVERPOOL
LIVERPOOL
YOU'LL NEVER WALK ALONE